NEEDLEPOINT
SAMPLERS

NEEDLEPOINT SAMPLERS

FELICITY LEWIS

STUDIO VISTA

STUDIO VISTA
an imprint of
Cassell
Villiers House,
41/47 Strand
London
WC2N 5JE

First published 1981
Reprinted 1987, 1990 (twice)
First paperback edition 1990

British Library Cataloguing in Publication Data
Lewis, Felicity
  Needlepoint samplers,
  1. Embroidery, Samplers
  I. Title
  746.44

  ISBN 0-289-80040-4

Typeset by Trident Graphics Limited
Printed in Hong Kong by
Colorcraft Ltd

Photographs: The photographs in the
Historical Introduction were all kindly
supplied by the Galleries or Museums
concerned. The photographs in Samplers
for Today were taken by Stephen Tanner,
with the exception of the following: cover,
title page, nos. 8, 10 and 15, which were
taken by David Lloyd.

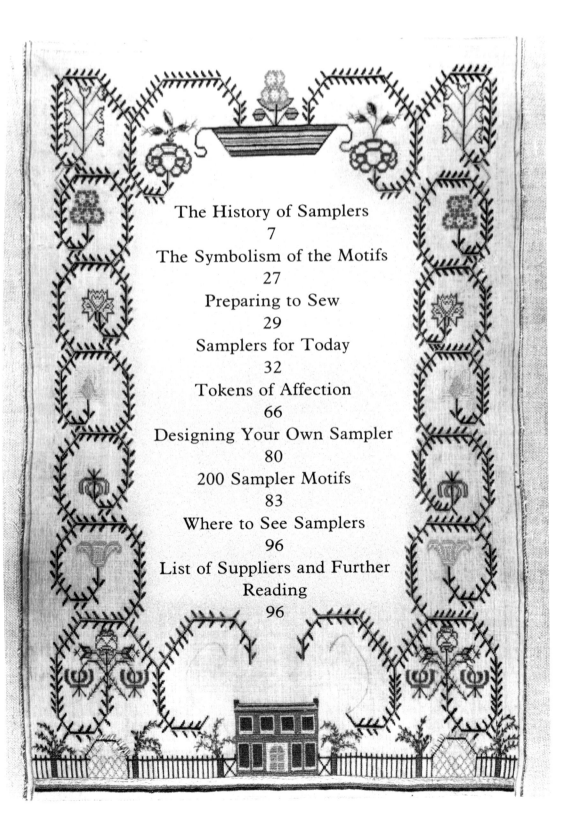

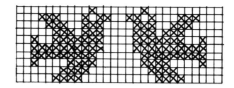

AUTHOR'S PREFACE

Having been interested in, and made a study of, samplers, particularly those of the 18th and 19th centuries, I, with the sampler workers of earlier days, would like to pass on some of my findings to others.

Now that the cost of acquiring original samplers is becoming prohibitive, I hope that the pages of graphed patterns taken from various museum collections and privately owned samplers, as well as the samplers and small 'tokens of affection' that I have devised, using these old motifs and border patterns, will all help to bring the simplicity and the liveliness of samplers to the notice of the needlewomen of today. It is inevitable that in translating these designs to coarser-meshed canvas the superb technical skill displayed in the minute stitches of earlier times will be lost, but I hope that some of the charm of the content of the sampler will have been retained, and that sampler workers of today will be inspired and helped by them.

You will find that I have used tent stitch throughout, but the samplers could be worked equally well in cross stitch. Should you prefer this approach, you can work the individual motifs in colour on a plain linen – there is no need to fill in all the background with stitching.

I should like to thank members of the staff of the following museums and collections who have enabled me to see the samplers in their care, and who have allowed me to make reference notes of designs and stitches – with a magnifying glass!

The American Museum in Britain, Bath
Birmingham City Museum
Blaise Castle Museum, Bristol
Bristol City Museum and Art Gallery
Cheltenham Museum
Fitzwilliam Museum, Cambridge
Gawthorpe Hall, (The Hon. R. B. Kay-Shuttleworth Trust), near Preston
Gloucester Folk Museum
Hereford City Museum
National Museum of Wales (St Fagan's), Cardiff
Sheffield City Museum
Snowshill Manor (The National Trust), near Broadway, Worcestershire
Stranger's Hall Museum, Norwich
Stroud Museum
Victoria and Albert Museum, London
Wells Museum
Worcester City Museum
York Castle Museum

I am also indebted to Mrs Ivy Parry for her help in preparing some of the samplers and Mrs Christine Livingstone for the final stitching together of the Tokens of Affection.

My thanks, too, to Mrs Joyce Cooper and Miss Barbara Bell for preparing the manuscript and to Miss Evelyn Rascopf of the New York Historical Society for her interest and assistance.

And, finally, to my sisters, Mrs Clarissa Rowland and Mrs Christine Mayer, for their encouragement and help in completing this project.

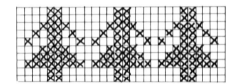

THE HISTORY OF SAMPLERS

The Origins of the Sampler

The first known samplers were worked in the 16th century, although they do not resemble the stylized piece of needlework that the word 'sampler' now brings to mind, and needlework, as an art form, flourished long before then – in the Middle Ages and even earlier. Double running stitch and pattern darning have been found in Coptic burial grounds in Egypt, and early embroidery in Europe reflects this Middle Eastern influence, with its use of the carnation and tulip as motifs. Embroiderers in this early time were professionals of both sexes and were employed both by the Church, for ecclesiastical garments and linens, and by the laity, for decoration of clothes and furnishings, as well as the marking and darning of linens.

With the Renaissance came a renewed interest in decoration in Europe, and embroidery was taken up by the amateur with great enthusiasm. Eager to try out new stitches and patterns, these adult needleworkers copied from each other, sewing the new stitches, before they could be forgotten, directly on to a piece of fabric. This fabric 'notebook' or memory jogger, sometimes very long, but rarely more than 23 cm (9 in) wide, was also used to try out a new stitch or pattern, sometimes inspired by an illuminated manuscript or church hanging. This long, thin piece of material became known as an *essamplaire*, from the French word meaning something to be copied or imitated, and was eventually anglicized as 'sampler'.

These early samplers were highly valued. They are mentioned in wills of the period and are included in royal inventories. They are unsigned, undated and often unfinished, and were intended as a reference tool rather than a decoration in themselves. In 1523 the first printed pattern books were produced at Augsburg in Germany, by Johann Sibmacher, and were followed quickly by pattern books printed in Italy, France and, later, England. Unfortunately, few of these pattern books survived, and the sampler therefore continued to be used as a reference tool until the 17th century.

1 A German sampler of 1704, with alphabets and decorative borders in blue and red only. *Museum of German Folk Art, Berlin.*

7

The 17th Century – the Golden Age of the Sampler

Throughout the 17th century many more stitches came into use. Samplers were now worked with silk and silver-gilt thread and workers experimented with all sorts of stitches, including Algerian eye or star stitch, Hungarian, Gobelin, Florentine, rococo, long-armed cross and eyelet stitches as well as the predominent tent and cross stitches. Samplers retained their long, narrow shape, with stitches or patterns worked in bands, or at random. The material used would be silk, either bleached or unbleached linen, or the yellow linen that was fashionable for collars and cuffs, and would be embroidered in coloured silks. Bands of cutwork included darning on net with buttonholing round the raw edges, so that when the threads of the ground were cut away a design made from buttonholing was left. Both the length of the sampler and the way in which various stitches were still informally jotted down on linen, suggest that the sampler continued to be used for reference well into the 17th century.

At the same time, young girls were being taught to work samplers purely as exercises in fine needlework, and throughout the 17th

and 18th centuries most girls between the ages of five and fifteen worked at least one during their schooldays. The school sampler became a piece of decorative embroidery, as well as providing practice.

Many examples from the 17th century happily survive today, and from these one can assume that samplers of that time fell into several categories. The largest group, mostly after 1629, consists of border patterns worked in silk, signed and dated. Many were in bright colours, worked with what a contemporary book describes as 'sundry sortes of spots, as Flowers, Birdes and Fishes, etc.'.

Another large group is cutwork samplers. Most of them are border patterns and single motifs taken from pattern books. The earliest English cutwork sampler in existence, signed and dated 1634, is displayed in the Museum of London. Embroidered with the arms of Queen Elizabeth, it suggests that the cutwork sampler was popular from the first part of the 17th century onwards. Cutwork was especially popular for the lace that was used lavishly on everything from clothes and accessories (ruffs, collars, cuffs, handkerchiefs) to all kinds of hangings and furnishings. Needlepoint lace and linen-thread cutwork was much in demand for edging, ruffs and caps. After 1625, when lace collars became the fashion, fine lace gradually replaced the cut and drawn sampler lace.

2 Sampler, 1660, with pulled thread work and spot motifs of carnation, Tudor Rose, butterflies, insects and geometric pattern work. A drawn outline shows a motif still to be sewn. *Bristol Museum and Art Gallery.*

3 17th century sampler showing bands of carnation, strawberry, acorn and rose borders and Tudor Rose and Boxer motifs, with an alphabet and drawn thread work. *Victoria and Albert Museum.*

4 This sampler of 1780 includes birds on a fruit tree and on flowers in pots, with stars, trees in urns, tulip, stag, lion, squirrel and owl, with a man and woman bearing baskets of fruit. *Victoria and Albert Museum.*

Schole-House, For the Needle, 1624: New and Singular Patternes and Workes of Linnen, the English edition of an Italian book, and Johann Sibmacher's *The Needle's Excellency.* The latter reached a twelfth edition by 1640 and his motifs, such as the dog and rabbit, parrot and spray of flowers, lady and gentleman, swan, are often found in English samplers. After 1650 the introduction of religious and moral inscriptions, which came to be recognized – however mistakenly – as an essential part of a sampler, signalled the end of the sampler as a pattern guide.

In Germany, two types of sampler were popular from the 17th century onwards. The first group were small samplers, featuring an alphabet and tiny geometric designs scattered at random. The second, like those of the same period in England, were long and narrow. They usually included several alphabets, border designs, a heraldic device,

such as a shield, containing a date and initials, and many scattered motifs, such as the Instruments of Passion, coronets, animals, birds, fruit trees and castles – all worked in cross stitch. Houses and domestic scenes do not, as a rule, appear. The most popular colour schemes were red, blue, green, yellow, tan and cream on tan linen.

Dutch samplers were similar in design to German ones of this period but different in shape and format, tending to be square or wider than they were long.

The 17th century was an age when the

Cut and drawn threadwork samplers were also extremely popular in Italy during this century. Worked on linen, and vertical in shape, they were greatly influenced by current styles and techniques in lace.

Denmark has some unusually fine examples of 'white work' samplers. White linen thread is used on white linen, creating a great variety of patterns in drawn and pulled work. Sweden also produced samplers copying the intricacies of lace. This 'white work' was used to decorate and embellish ruffles, fichus, aprons and suchlike.

Samplers were frequently embroidered in white linen thread, the patterns being derived from lace pattern books and showing Italian influence. Sometimes the white linen thread was used in conjunction with coloured silks and/or cutwork.

In the school samplers, alphabets began to appear. These letters were used for marking linen, and it was necessary for a girl to prepare for future household tasks. No numerals appear on samplers until the middle of the 17th century, but after this they were also needed for marking linen and were thus practised on samplers.

As the long rolled-up sampler gradually disappeared, pattern books took their place, for example Richard Shorleyker's *A*

knowledge of a wide range of patterns, stitches and motifs was a necessity, for needlework was an everyday art. One English sampler, dated 1681, contains cross, back and satin stitch, herringbone, double-running, basket, hem, outline and Algerian eye stitches. The long, narrow shape of samplers remained popular, while the spontaneous charm of quickly recorded ideas and patterns scattered at random gave way to ordered, horizontal bands of embroidery. Geometrics, stylized flowers and alphabets continued to be much in evidence. The acorn and the Tudor Rose were featured and many other flower designs such as the columbine, thistle, cornflower and pansy, were taken from herbals and contemporary books on gardening.

Popular figures were 'the boxers', so called because they always appeared with arms raised, one of them holding a trophy which varied from a vase to a spray with leaves, branches, a four-petalled flower or candelabra. Rather than real boxers, they were possibly the Greek *erotes* or Roman *amores*, or even the Cupids of the Renaissance, but in any case these figures, always clothed, were popular for over a hundred years.

Other samplers are packed with motifs which hang together thematically. Animals were very popular, as were fruits and flowers. In the first half of the century the predominant colours were natural greens, pale yellows, creams, browns, a little blue, red, dark purple and through to black. After 1650, colours became brighter and richer, and more solid effects were achieved with the use of tent and satin stitch.

Although the 17th century was the 'Golden Age' of the sampler, there are very few samplers surviving from before 1648. Earlier samplers would seem to have been destroyed

5 This brightly-coloured cross stitch sampler on natural linen canvas is by a boy, and may depict a Quaker seminary. *The Embroiderers' Guild.*

6 A German sampler of 1704, with random motifs of birds, flowers, animals and crowns. *Museum of German Folk Art, Berlin.*

7 A Dutch sampler of the 18th century showing a ship, tulips in pots and domestic scenes as well as alphabets and crowns. *Rijksmuseum, Amsterdam.*

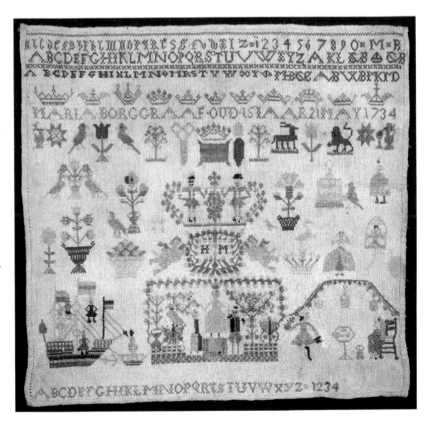

8 18th century Dutch sampler with Dutch house, and flower and leaf border. *Rijksmuseum, Amsterdam.*

9 A finely worked sampler of 1791 containing a variety of alphabets separated by geometric strip patterns, bands of strawberries and carnations and various crowns. *Birmingham Museum and Art Gallery.*

10 Sampler by Mary Hall in 1800, on homespun wool. *New York Historical Society.*

11 Sampler, 1814, with bands of alphabets, numerals and flowers in urns either side of trees and, perhaps, the home of the sewer. *Bristol Museum and Art Gallery.*

either by moths or the Puritans. Those which did survive are mostly on coarse linen, suggesting that perhaps the moths are more to be blamed than the Puritans!

Samplers arrived in North America with the *Mayflower*. Easily transportable, the sampler served as a sentimental link with home, a decoration and a necessary reference work. The colonists had to master the arts of spinning, weaving and dyeing their own crops of flax or hemp, and the resulting linen, used for the ground of the very earliest American samplers, was often coarse and unbleached. The thread used also had to be home-spun and dyed, limiting the range of colours to those naturally accessible from trees, roots and berries.

As their crops flourished, however, trade with the Old World began and expanded. Fabrics were imported from Europe, adding variety to the home-made linens and to the restricted colours available hitherto.

However, the American sampler in the 17th century was so much influenced by English embroidery that it could not really be described as American, with a style and character of its own. Although the long, narrow shape of the English samplers of this period never really gained popularity in America, the bands of conventionalized motifs were typically English.

As people became more prosperous, their good fortune was reflected in their samplers. A first sampler, for example, might be sewn with red cotton and a second worked with finer silks and materials.

The 18th Century

By the 18th century, the sampler had almost completely lost its reference value and had become much more of a practical exercise in embroidery. There was less need for economy of material and consequently samplers became square. In English samplers, motifs were arranged symmetri-

cally in the centre of the sampler, surrounded by a border of floral or geometric patterns. Worthy of being framed and admired – and as objects of permanent interest – they recorded important family events such as births, marriages and deaths. Family trees and almanacs, alphabets and inscriptions were included, as well as names and dates. Band patterns gave way to neat arrangements of small motifs: pairs of ornamental flowers in pots, baskets of fruit, trees and animals, sometimes with landscape scenes at the base, incorporating human figures and a house. The influence of imported Indian cottons was strong and designs became more naturalistic. Pyramid trees were doubtless inspired by the topiary of the time.

Colours became brighter and less naturalistic. Carnations and honeysuckle were still popular flower motifs, trees, animals, birds and fruit were still regularly included, but another motif emerged as one of the most popular in sampler history, the crown or coronet, often a whole collection of them, with an initial to denote the title each represented. Such crowns or coronets were often used to mark the property of the nobility for whom the sewer – as a maid – might easily work in the future.

In Holland, from the 18th to the 19th century, samplers tended to have small leaf or conventionalized flower borders framing a host of individual motifs arranged at random. A typical Dutch house was often included, surrounded by dogs, deer, birds, vases of flowers, coronets, heraldic devices and a woman by a gate, sometimes holding a broom, to symbolize the housewife. As befits a sailing nation, a sailing ship with people on the rigging often features prominently, the number of figures perhaps signifying the number of people in the embroiderer's family.

In some ways, the Dutch samplers were very much like the English samplers of the same period. Worked mostly in cross stitch, they were perhaps technically inferior to

Three 19th century English samplers, all with flower borders surrounding text and motifs. 12 includes stags and a parrot. *The National Trust, Snowshill Manor, Worcs.*, 13 is a formal arrangement of decorative motifs in delightful colours. *Private collection*, 14 shows sun, moon and stars and a rustic scene in which the sewer herself appears. *Wells Museum.*

12

14

13

15 German sampler of 1741 with Adam and Eve, grape bearers and many other motifs, and various borders. *Museum of German Folk Art, Berlin.*

samplers of other countries, but they showed possibly more creative flair and charm than most.

In contrast, Italian samplers of this period, although showing a high standard of workmanship, lacked the natural spontaneity of earlier work. Usually wider than they were long, they contained flowers, furniture and trees and often the Instruments of Passion, surrounded by unobtrusive borders. More often than not, the samplers were signed and dated by the embroiderer. The embroidery was worked in silks of all colours on cream linen, predominantly in cross stitch, although satin, chain, feather, stem and double running stitch also appear.

French samplers, with their square or horizontal shape and almost exclusive use of cross stitch, are reminiscent of the Italian

16 Alphabets, verse, name and date enclosed in a lozenge shape, surrounded by a free floral border. 1821. *Birmingham Museum and Art Gallery.*

17 A series of designs in rows includes trees, a verse and floral motifs with a child's name enclosed by a garland of leaves at the base. *Welsh Folk Museum, Cardiff.*

and the Dutch samplers. They usually contained a border round all four sides, of more interest than their Italian counterparts, and carried the usual European motifs – the Instruments of Passion being one example. A verse embroidered in the shape of a shield also often occurs.

Spanish and Mexican samplers have much in common. Although there is evidence that they were made as early as the 16th century, few have survived from before the 18th century. The embroidery is superb, worked in silks of many colours on white linen, or in bright or darker colours such as blue, tan and brown on white or brown linen. Satin stitch was used predominantly. Some also exist simply in black and white – a very popular colour scheme in Spanish households.

Spanish samplers were either rectangular or square, some with a central motif enclosed in a square, usually named and dated. Border motifs of different widths included geometric and floral patterns. A few samplers displayed alphabets, texts, verses or numerals. In some, cut and drawn work was combined with bands of designs. Most of the samplers made in Mexico were rectangular with random designs which often included animals and birds but seldom a central motif.

It was in the 18th century that samplers became more pictorial. Biblical scenes were often to be found – Adam and Eve and the return of the spies from Canaan were the two most constant favourites, popular in Holland as well as England.

In America, about the middle of the century, the pictorial element often took the form of a landscape across the bottom of the sampler, typically small mounds or hills with trees or flowers growing from their peaks and birds and animals scattered above. This form of sampler continued well into the 19th century, developing into a true landscape, often very naturalistic in character. The English influence gradually died away, until at the end of the century

18 A centrally placed verse name and date, enclosed by a carnation border, with patterns of flowers in baskets and with trees above and below. 1829. *Welsh Folk Museum, Cardiff.*

19 An unusual sampler in which lettering gives way to formal arrangements of a house, trees, flowers in pots and fruit in baskets, and a rustic scene at the base. *Birmingham Museum and Art Gallery.*

American samplers could be said to have a true character of their own.

Inscriptions on English samplers became longer and more elaborate. Familiar texts were verses from the Bible, the Lord's Prayer, the Creed and the Ten Commandments: moral thoughts, often somewhat morbid, abounded, and the great hymn writers, such as Wesley, were much quoted, in the hope that the young sewers absorbed the precepts as they stitched. As inscriptions became longer, the variety of stitches decreased for lack of space.

In American samplers, family records were popular from about 1737. The record was usually centred on the sampler and surrounded by a border. Traditionally, coloured silks were used to embroider the names of those who were alive, and black for the dead.

Two new phenomena in sampler-making, darning and holliepoint, occurred in the 18th century, recalling the samplers of earlier centuries.

The former, popular in England, America, Germany and Holland, was the means by which a child learnt how to darn. They required very fine, counted thread-work on the muslin, cambric or damask fabrics used for the dresses of the period. Sometimes holes were cut and then filled in with very neat darns or cross stitch. An interesting pattern would be created where the horizontal threads met.

Holliepoint is like needlepoint lace, but the patterns were made by leaving out stitches. Typical designs were flowers or simple geometrical patterns, names, dates and mottoes, worked on linen with linen thread. Holliepoint lace was used in shirts, and in gowns and caps for babies.

20 A charmingly individual arrangement of verses and rustic scenes, 1788. *Gloucester Folk Museum.*

21 This sampler, sewn by Ann Sophia Page, aged 7, shows how an inexperienced hand may produce a really individual work of art. *Bristol Museum and Art Gallery.*

Proverbs. Chap. VIII. ver. 33

Hear. instruction and be wise and

Refuse it not.

ANN × SOPHIA × PAGE
AGED 7 YEARS

ROYAL OAK

ABCDEFGHIJKLMNOPQRSTUVWXYZ&

A variety of materials, including satin and fine wool, were used for the base fabric of samplers, but linen was still the most popular.

Towards the end of the century, the working of map samplers helped girls to learn geography, and in America, at the Quaker Westtown School in Pennsylvania, the girls embroidered not only maps but globes, worked in silk thread on a silk fabric.

By the end of the century there was, it would seem, no further need for economy and the average size of the sampler was about 33–46 cm (13–18 in) long by 25–33 cm (10–13 in) wide. But there were still the occasional long and narrow samplers. There were also charming small

samplers, anything from 5–12.5 cm (2–5 in) square, which were made into small gifts, such as needle and letter cases.

The flowerpot, bird, animal and Adam and Eve motifs appeared less often, as did the use of beads and metal thread. It was during this period that the use of human hair, instead of thread, became fashionable. Silk threads became more vivid in colour, and showed a greater variety of shades than those of the 17th century. Colours employed in darning samplers tended to be more subtle, but numerals and alphabets were worked in many different colours. Longer inscriptions were usually embroidered in one colour only – red or black – and in the second half of the century some

23

24

23

25

22 19th century Dutch sampler with variety of flower motifs and dovecote, centre top. *Rijksmuseum, Amsterdam.*

23 This sampler in black cross stitch is by a 6 year old. Pious texts and oak tree motifs are surrounded with a border and unusual arrangement of letters on all four sides. *The National Trust, Snowshill Manor, Worcs.*

24 This long sampler includes horses, cows, birds in cages among a variety of motifs and, possibly, the Seminary alluded to under the verses. *Birmingham Museum and Art Gallery.*

25 A lady with a basket of fruit on her head, her dog, and a tree in an urn, appear either side of a house, with verse and border patterns. *Welsh Folk Museum, Cardiff.*

were worked entirely in black silk.

In Germany, during the 18th century, two other types of sampler using just one or two colours became popular. Around Hamburg, samplers were embroidered predominantly in cream and black silk in cross stitch on cream linen. They usually contained an alphabet, the name of the embroiderer, the date the sampler was worked, and scattered conventionalized hearts, flowers and coronets. The second type were worked in red cotton on white linen, using a variety of stitches including satin, stem, hem, filling and eyelet stitch.

In America, the end of the 18th century saw the development of fully embroidered canvasses, with the background covered with satin or other stitches. Stitches themselves became more elaborate, as in the unusual rococo stitch.

In England, however, the number of stitches used had decreased to such an extent by 1800 that by then most samplers were entirely worked in cross stitch.

The 19th Century

The standard of needlework of most 19th-century samplers is generally considered to be inferior to that of the 18th century, but superb examples of workmanship are to be found among the great variety of formats that abound.

Some samplers show symmetrical, well-spaced arrangements of trees, flowers in pots, birds and other motifs, grouped round a central inscription or verse, the whole surrounded on four sides by a border. In others, the space round the central area, often featuring a house, Adam and Eve or an inscription, was crammed haphazardly with a plethora of spot motifs, the border giving form to the whole.

Many samplers depict delightful sprays of flowers, with birds, leaves, tendrils and bows framing the pious verses or alphabets in the centre. School samplers show simple arrangements of alphabets and numerals, separated by zigzag bands of stitches, with the sewer's name and date beneath, and sometimes, a few motifs, such as flowers in pots, birds or trees. Often the sampler has a plain line of stitches forming a border all round. Registers with dates of births, marriages and deaths of members of a family were popular, and could be very decorative.

In England, the colours most frequently used in samplers of this period were pale pink, brick- and rust-red, pale, mid- and dull-blue, dark prussian blue, tan, curry-brown, olive-green and shades of grey and black, but some are worked in brighter tones. The majority of the samplers were worked on woollen canvas or linen, a coarse, unbleached variety being popular from 1830–50.

Plain sewing was taught in charity schools and orphanages, where the children were expected to mark numerous handkerchiefs and all the bedlinen. Cross stitch was

22

26 Some of the bird and tree designs in this lively sampler have a very modern look. 1847. *Welsh Folk Museum, Cardiff.*

27 Lucretia Bright embroidered her family tree quite literally in this American sampler, *courtesy of the Daughters of the American Revolution.*

28 A German sampler of 1859, with alphabets, numerals and motifs in bright colours. *Museum of German Folk Art, Berlin.*

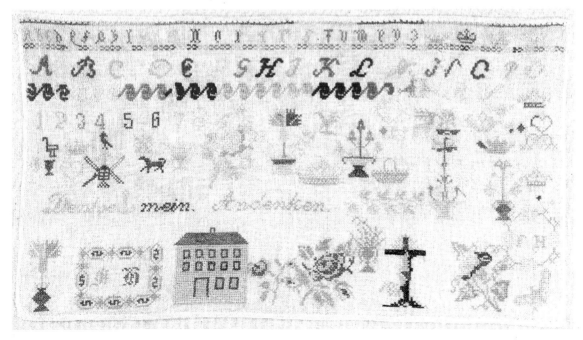

29

30

31

29 This shows the amazing technical skill of a child at an orphanage in 1867. *Bristol Museum and Art Gallery.*

30 Berlin work patterns influenced these 3-dimensional flowers, churches, animals (including elephant and tiger) and rustic scenes. Undated. *Victoria and Albert Museum.*

31 Dutch sampler with Adam and Eve, serpent and fruit tree, the Dutch Lion in the Garden of Holland and the Dutch or Free Maiden signifying liberty, and the Tree of Life flanked by birds and stags. *Welsh Folk Museum, Cardiff.*

32 Work-bag with very decorative motifs including mice and windmill. *Fitzwilliam Museum, Cambridge.*

the main stitch involved. The price list of 'plain work' produced by the School of Industry, Cheltenham, where such garments as nightcaps and neck handkerchiefs were made up, includes the following items:

Marking each ....a letter ½d
Ditto each ....a figure ¼d

In Berlin in the early 19th century, a completely new form of needlework appeared. The rather florid patterns were printed in colour on squared paper, making them extremely easy for the embroiderer to follow. The wools sold to accompany them were brightly coloured, even garish, including colours never before available, such as magenta, violet and mauve.

The craze for Berlin woolwork spread rapidly across Europe and to Russia, England and America, and remained popular until the close of the century. It was usually worked in cross or tent stitch, but sometimes silk, chenille and beads were included. Motifs included alphabets, children, animals, birds, flowers and temples, treated in a very naturalistic way. Shading and three-dimensional affects were

possible due to the wide range of colour tones available.

Samplers worked on wool and linen, with the usual arrangements of alphabet, numerals and borders, continued to emerge from schools until the end of the century and into the early years of the 20th century, but they were also made in Berlin wool on coarser canvas and these tended to look very garish in colour and clumsy in design.

In Holland, apart from the introduction of the Berlin work samplers, styles remained similar to those of the previous century. In France, the trend was for landscape samplers, similar to those which appeared in England and America in the early part of the 19th century. A typical scene would include a French house, trees and people.

In America, borders changed from the earlier angular and conventionalized designs of roses, carnations and strawberries to more naturalistic sprays of flowers and leaves which reflected the nature of American gardens. This style of border was quite different from the stylized borders on English samplers, which continued to be popular in the early part of the century. The American samplers of this period showed a striking individuality and creative talent, but technically they remained inferior to those produced in England.

As in other countries, religious groups ran schools in America's early days, the Quakers and Moravians being especially noted for their attention to needlework in the curriculum. In Pennsylvania, where both of these denominations were active, a somewhat regional flavour was established, the city of Philadelphia being renowned for samplers sewn on a dark green ground, using threads of white, cream, yellow and pink. Darning samplers were also sewn on the same green.

Pennsylvanian samplers, made by embroiderers of Dutch or German descent, relate more closely to the European tradition than any others made in America. The landscape sampler, so popular in other parts of America, never appeared here. Motifs were angular and stylized, and included peacocks, square-topped hearts, coronets, six-pointed stars and flowers with straight stems growing in vases. These samplers rarely had borders, but they often had a ribbon binding round the edge and sometimes a ribbon rosette in the corners.

Towards the latter half of the 19th century, apart from Berlin work very few samplers were made and these were not of the finer quality of earlier years. Perhaps, as in so many spheres of the arts, the Industrial Revolution is to blame. With machines to reproduce patterns and wools in cheap, garish colours, the results were lifeless, though those embroidered in cotton and silk were more attractive than those worked in wool.

Most samplers had a border on all four sides, often consisting of carnation or strawberry motifs. Some beads were used, and in some samplers the house of the workers was depicted. Dated, with signatures and inscriptions, the favourite motifs continued to be birds, pets and flowers in pots, and these were also used to decorate small objects in daily use, such as 'housewifes' – rolled-up sewing kits – spectacle cases and small workbags.

Gradually the still, lifeless look of the Berlin woolwork had taken a hold, and samplers never again seemed to regain their individual charm.

The 20th Century

Very little good sampler work has been done, so far, in this century. The gentle pace of the 19th-century household gave way to a different sort of life for the leisured classes. Embroidery was no longer a top priority subject for the schoolgirl, and although school samplers were worked until 1920 they were of an elementary standard. Worked in cross stitch, in wool, standard cotton or crochet silk, they were mostly embroidered on dingy yellow, open-meshed canvas or linen. The designs were usually dreary rows of alphabets and numerals, rather like a marking sampler, though some showed simple bird and animal patterns and baskets of fruit.

A number of low-priced embroidery magazines were published during these years, supplying patterns and instructions. Designs on the whole were dull and uncreative – stereotyped birds, animals and baskets of fruit – in no way equal to the delightful and exquisitely made samplers of earlier times.

But since the 1950s people have once again shown a renewed interest and pride in reproducing traditional crafts, and samplers have become highly prized collectors' items.

33 A souvenir pin cushion from the Cheltenham School of Industry, cross stitch on linen. *Cheltenham Museum.*

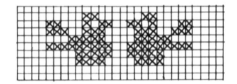

THE SYMBOLISM
OF THE MOTIFS

Most of the animals, birds, flowers and other motifs which appear on samplers have an historical or religious significance.

lion strength, steadfastness, courage and hope. In Dutch samplers the Garden of Holland, symbol of the House of Orange, is seen enclosed by a fence, with the Dutch lion holding a sword in its right paw and a bunch of arrows in its left

stag or hart gentleness and pride

dog fidelity and watchfulness

squirrel mischief

spinning monkey folly, laziness, lechery and vanity: in Dutch samplers is a symbol of the Devil

pelican piety, and signifies death and resurrection

parrot talkativeness and gossip

peacock ostentation, vanity and luxury: can also be a symbol of gracious demeanour and of immortality

owl wisdom, but also used to symbolize the Devil or the demon of avarice

swan the bird of love, also represents a good death, because it sings sweetly while dying: also an emblem of the Lutheran Church

eagle the national emblem of America appears almost exclusively on American samplers

dove charity, mercy and peace

cock watchfulness and penitence

bee hope, the beehive being an emblem of the monastic or church community

butterfly and moth inconstancy, immortality, joy, playfulness and pleasure

the Tree of Life one of the commonest motifs on samplers, sometimes flanked by the figures of Adam and Eve, or by animals and birds

weeping willow the sorrow and dejection of the bereaved; refers particularly to the early death of Princess Charlotte, only child of George IV

fruit tree the apple was an ancient symbol of love and fertility because of its sweetness, as was the basket of fruit: in Christian art, it represents temptation and evil: the number of apples depicted is usually about fifteen: in some Armenian samplers seven apples represent the seven deadly sins

lily purity and innocence

rose pagan symbol for love

violet or daisy humility

wild pansy, or trinity violet these two humble flowers were favourites of Queen Elizabeth I of England

honeysuckle traditionally connected with averting the evil eye

carnation poverty and love

tulip appears most frequently in Dutch samplers as a symbol of perfect love

strawberries, honeysuckle and **acorns** figure frequently in the borders of samplers, as the shape of the flowers, leaves and stems lend themselves to decorative treatment

man often depicted with a bird perched on his hand, the male figure signifies marital fidelity

woman frequently seen holding a palm

branch, the female figure is a symbol of life

man and woman together, often holding a garland, the two figures symbolize marriage

the spies of Canaan or grapebearers these two figures represented Joshua and Caleb, spies sent by Moses into Canaan: they also symbolize the Jews and Gentiles: the hanging grapes refer to Christ crucified

house often the home of the embroiderer, or if the sampler was sewn by a young person, the school

chairs diligence, hospitality and domesticity

windmill found mainly in Dutch samplers, windmills are often shown in country scenes together with livestock

ship hope, or the soul's voyage to a safe haven, and also a marriage emblem

crown eternity and fidelity: crowns and coronets, denoting ranks of the nobility, appeared on marked linen

heart divine love

stars the eight-pointed star is an emblem of Bethlehem, the six-pointed star is a Jewish symbol, and the five-pointed star announced the birth of Christ

square and octagon both symbols of Nature

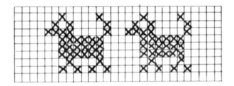

PREPARING TO SEW

All the samplers and 'Tokens of Affection' in this book have been worked with wool on canvas in tent stitch, but they could just as easily be worked in cross stitch.

Canvas There are two types of canvas, single-thread and double-thread, or Penelope, canvas, both of which are measured by the number of threads (or double-threads) to the 2.5 cm (1 in). The samplers and tokens I have devised have been worked on single-thread canvas, 14 threads to 2.5 cm (1 in), double-thread canvas, 11 threads to 2.5 cm (1 in), and a few items on much finer canvas, 18 threads to 2.5 cm (1 in).

Thread The basic threads for canvas embroidery are tapestry wool and crewel wool. Crewel wool is a fine 2-ply wool, and the number of strands used can be varied according to the fineness of the canvas. Tapestry wool is a thicker 4-ply wool and is used as a single thread. Tapestry wool tends to wear thin if too long a thread is used when sewing; a length of about 30 cm (12 in) is a good working length.

Grounding wool for working backgrounds can be bought in larger skeins and comes in a variety of shades.

Needles Tapestry needles have blunt ends and come in various sizes to suit the canvas and thread used.

Frames Embroidery frames (see fig. 3) can be square or rectangular and come in various sizes, determined by the length of the webbing on the rollers. A 65 cm (26 in) frame is a good one to start on, as it is a useful size and easy to manage. A round tambour frame is not suitable for this kind of embroidery. Many of the small articles in this book were sewn in the hand and not on a frame, but it is advisable to use a frame for larger items or the canvas may pull out of shape and the stitching become uneven. It is also a good idea to sew several smaller items on the same piece of canvas, using a frame. Allow at least 4 cm (1½ in) from the edges of the canvas, and leave about 7.5 cm (3 in) between two items, so that when they are all completed, removed from the frame and cut apart, each one will have about 4 cm (1½ in) of unsewn canvas surrounding the worked areas.

Preparing the canvas for a 65 cm (26 in) frame Always use the canvas with the selvedge vertical. Never work the canvas the wrong way as this not only affects the look of the stitches, but makes it impossible to match the edges when you make up the article.

Cut the canvas 48 cm (19 in) in height by 61 cm (24 in) wide. Mark the centre top of the canvas. Cut off the selvedge from the sides. Tack lines of stitches through the centre of the canvas, vertically and horizontally, using a fine cotton thread. Turn in

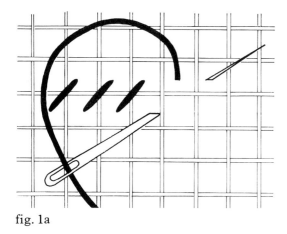

fig. 1a

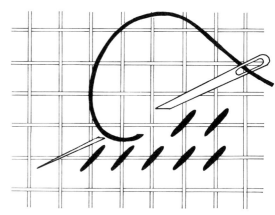

fig. 1b

1.5 cm (½ in) at the top and bottom and tack on the wrong side. Turn and tack the two sides in the same way and then bind them with 2.5 cm (1 in) wide tape or webbing.

Framing up the canvas (see fig. 3) With right sides together and matching centres carefully, pin and then tack the canvas to the webbing (C) on one roller (A), working from the centre out. Oversew the edges with strong thread. Repeat for second roller. Slip the ends of the two arms (B) through the slots in the rollers and extend the frame until the canvas is taut, but not too tight.

Now lace the two sides of the canvas to the arms. One way of doing this is to use string or carpet thread and a packing needle, and to sew through the taped edge (D) and around the arm of the frame at intervals of about 2.5 cm (1 in). Use a length of about 2.75 m (3 yd) of thread, and work from the centre to the sides, allowing about 46 cm (18 in) at each end for securing to the frame.

For another method you will need about 2.75 m (3 yd) of 1.5 cm (½ in) width tape. Pin the centre of the tape to the centre of the taped edge of the canvas. Then, working from the centre out, take the tape around the arm and pin it to the canvas at 4 cm (1½ in) intervals. Attach the ends securely to the frame.

You will find it is necessary to tighten the string or tape from time to time as you work, to keep the canvas taut, and thus keep your work in good shape and your stitches regular.

The canvas is now ready to be worked.

Tent stitch Tent stitch (see fig. 1) is one of the simplest embroidery stitches: its smaller version is known as petit point. Bring the thread up at the left-hand side of the canvas, take the needle back and down over one thread and bring it up two threads further on. Continue until the first row is complete, then work the second row right to left, taking the needle back over one thread and forward under two. Work backwards and forwards in this way, completely covering the canvas. When this stitch is worked correctly, the stitches on the reverse side are long and sloping.

Left-handed people can work the same stitch in the opposite direction, so that it slopes from top left to bottom right rather than top right to bottom left. Some of the samplers and tokens in the following pages have been worked left-handed to illustrate this.

Cross stitch For cross stitch, work a row of slanting stitches from left to right and then work another row, right to left on top of them – do not work individual crosses one at a time. Each cross must be worked over an equal number of threads, down and across, and the top stitches must always lie in the same direction (see fig. 2).

Stretching If you have worked your sampler in the hand, not on a frame, and it has pulled out of shape, it will be necessary to stretch it. Never press canvas work with an iron, as this flattens the texture. Cover a wooden board with two or three sheets of blotting paper and lay the work face down on top of it. Dampen the back of the embroidery with a cloth, then remove it and dampen the blotting paper. Place the work back over the blotting paper, right side up. Position one of the selvedges flush with

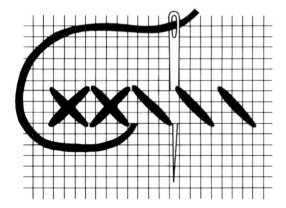

fig. 2

the edge of the board and gently pull the work into shape, squaring the corners. Pin it firmly to the board. Use rustless drawing pins or tack, and do not pin too near the edge of the embroidery. Leave in position on the board for about 24 hours, away from heat, until completely dry and in shape.

Finishing off There are two ways of finishing off a sampler, depending on how it is to be framed or hung. To produce simple neatened edges, cut off the extra canvas to

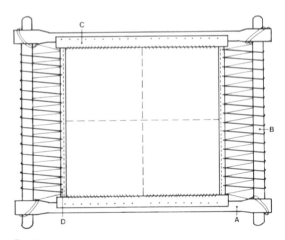

fig. 3

within about 2 cm (¾ in) of the finished embroidery, turn the canvas under at each corner and pin it down firmly. Turn under the remaining canvas, making sure that on the right side, the edges of the embroidery appear quite straight and that no spare canvas shows. The corners must be sharp and neat. Pin the turned-in canvas in position, then oversew all the edges to the back of the work. The sampler can now be inserted in a frame.

Lacing over a board enables the sampler to be hung directly on the wall, or placed in a frame. Cut a piece of hardboard 6 mm (¼ in) smaller all round than the stitched area of the sampler. Lay the sampler over the board, centring it carefully. Fold the edges of the canvas round to the back of the board. Using strong thread, start lacing opposite edges to each other, beginning in the centre and working out towards the corners. Use close herringbone stitches and pull them up tightly and evenly. Check as you work that the sampler stays in the correct position over the board. Complete two opposite sides before starting the other two. Finish the thread ends off securely.

SAMPLERS FOR TODAY

The following sampler designs have not, unless otherwise stated, been based on any one particular piece of needlework, but have been devised using reference notes from samplers of different periods.

The colours used are suggestions only. The range of shades in which tapestry wool or thread is produced nowadays is very wide, and you may like to choose colours to tone with the furnishings of a particular room.

The canvas used is either double thread, 11 threads to 2.5 cm (1 in); single thread, 14 threads to 2.5 cm (1 in); or single thread, 18 threads to 2.5 cm (1 in).

1 Sampler showing peacocks and butterfly enclosed in a border, above numerals and date in a garland, surrounded by a variety of motifs. Seven colours on cream ground. Single thread canvas, 14 threads to the inch. Size 9¾″×8¾″ (24.8×22.2 cm).

32

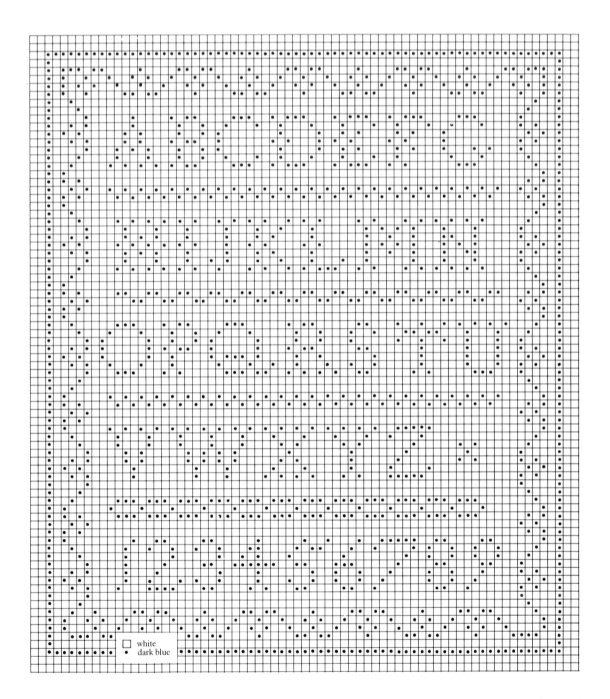

white
dark blue

2 Sampler without lettering, consisting of a symmetrical arrangement of trees, birds, dogs and flowers, surrounded by a strawberry border. Four colours on cream ground. Double thread canvas, 11 threads to the inch. Size 10¼″×12½″ (26×31.8 cm).

3 Small sampler with alphabet, border and numerals in one colour on white ground. Based on a small version on linen in Worcester City Museum. Single thread canvas, 14 threads to the inch. Size 5¾″×5″ (14.6×12.7 cm).

4 Sampler depicting Adam and Eve and the Tree of Knowledge, with angels, crowns, stags, and baskets of fruit surrounded by an acorn border. Eleven colours on a beige ground. Double thread canvas, 11 threads to the inch. Size 14½″×14½″ (36.8×36.8 cm).

5 Sampler with alphabet, numerals, name and date, with trees, birds, baskets of fruit and ornamental trees and a plain border. Seven colours on a beige ground. Double thread canvas, 11 threads to the inch. Size 10¼″×11⅝″ (26×30 cm).

red
dark green
light brown
royal blue
light green
plum
pale pink
beige

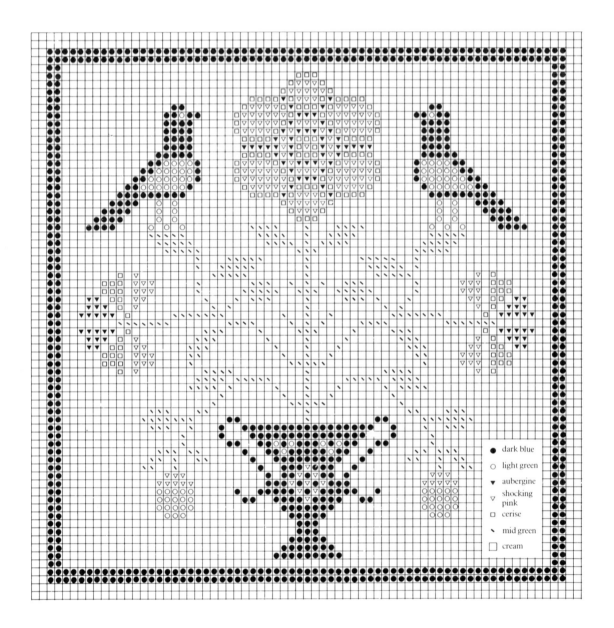

6 Sampler with alphabet, man and woman and small motifs. Seven colours on beige ground. Double thread canvas, 11 threads to the inch. Size 8″×10¾″ (20.3×27.3 cm).

7 Sampler without lettering, showing birds perching on a flower in a pot. Six colours on a cream ground. Double thread canvas, 11 threads to the inch. Size 7″×7″ (17.8×17.8 cm).

43

ABCDEFGH
IJKLMNOP
QRSTUVW
XYZ

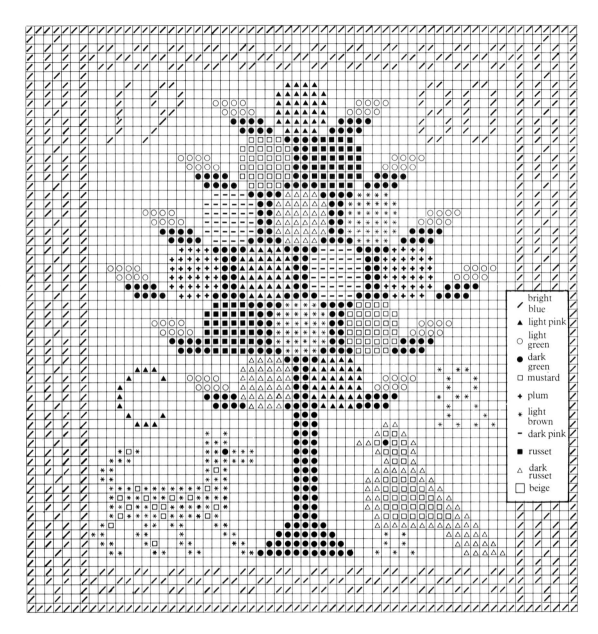

8 Small sampler with initials, date, dog, bird and fruit tree, within a border. Based on a sampler in York Castle Museum which was without letters or numerals. Ten colours on a beige ground. Single thread canvas, 14 threads to the inch. Size 4⅝″ × 4⅞″ (11.7 × 12.4 cm).

46

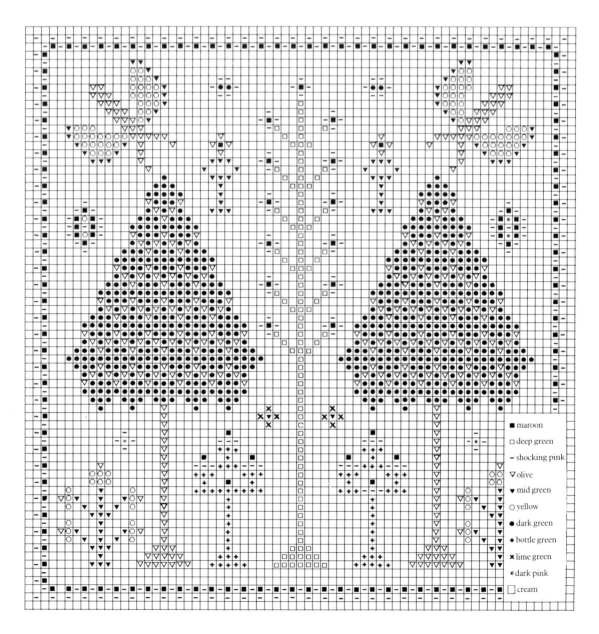

9 Sampler without lettering, showing butterflies and trees with a simple border. Ten colours on cream ground. Double thread canvas, 11 threads to the inch. Size 6¾″×6⅞″ (17.1×17.5 cm).

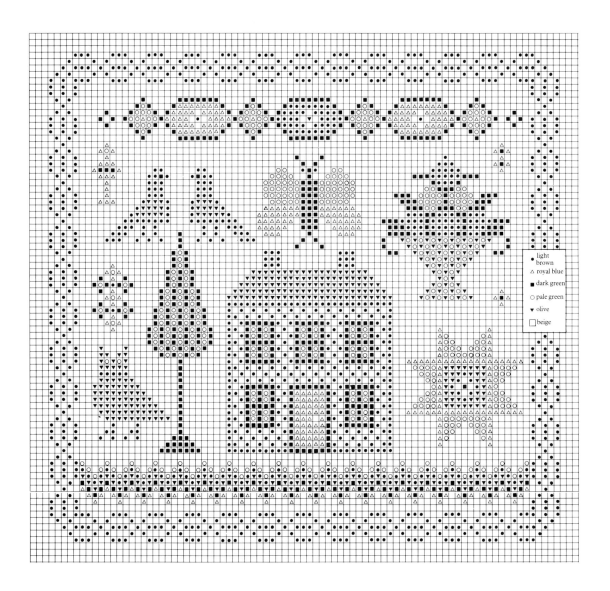

The legend within the chart reads:

- • light brown
- △ royal blue
- ■ dark green
- ○ pale green
- ▼ olive
- □ beige

10 Sampler without lettering. Five colours on a beige ground. Double thread canvas, 11 threads to the inch. Size 8⁷⁄₈″×8³⁄₁₆″ (22.5×21 cm).

11 Sampler with the wording 'Make Much of Time', name and numerals. Seven colours on cream ground. Double thread canvas, 11 threads to the inch. Size 7″×10″ (17.8×25.4 cm).

Make much of time

Charity Bowland '81

12 Sampler in which a strawberry border surrounds alphabets and a country scene of three figures, sheep, dogs, birds, trees and deer. Twenty-three colours on cream ground. Single thread canvas, 14 threads to the inch. Size 11⅛″×10½″ (28.3×26.7 cm).

13 Sampler showing birds on a tree, numerals, dogs, sheep etc., initials and date with a strawberry border. Eight colours on a cream ground. Single thread canvas, 14 threads to the inch. Size 6¾″×8⅝″ (17.1×21.9 cm).

● mid green
○ bright pink
▲ purple
□ russet
△ dark blue
— light brown
■ olive
∗ mustard
□ cream

14 Sampler showing a house flanked by trees, dogs and floral motifs, with space for initials and date to be inserted, surrounded by a carnation border. Ten colours on a cream ground. Single thread canvas, 18 threads to the inch, for which stranded thread must be used. Size 9⅛" × 13½" (23.2 × 34.3 cm).

gold
dark green
black
fawn
royal blue
mid brown
light brown
shocking pink
beige

15 Sampler with
alphabet, verse and
border patterns, dogs,
trees, stars, baskets of
fruit and floral motifs.
Based on a sampler in
Hereford City
Museum. Eight
colours on beige
ground. Single thread
canvas, 14 threads to
the inch. Size
15½″×15″
(39.4×38.1 cm).

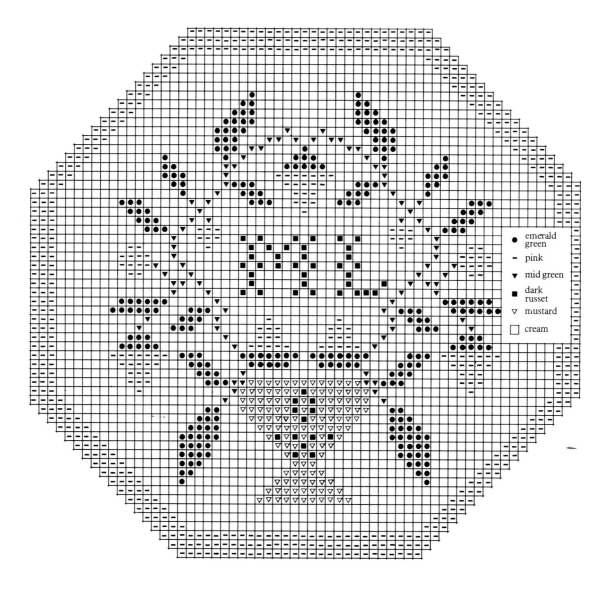

The legend within the chart:

- ● emerald green
- − pink
- ▼ mid green
- ■ dark russet
- ▽ mustard
- ☐ cream

16 Octagonal sampler showing initials in a garland. Five colours on cream ground. Double thread canvas, 11 threads to the inch. Size 6″×6¼″ (15.2×15.8 cm): length of each edge approximately 2½″–2¾″ (6.4–7 cm).

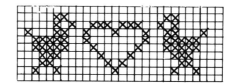

TOKENS OF AFFECTION

In the 17th century, old reference samplers which had been superseded by new ones were cut up into sections and used to make small objects such as needlecases and pincushions.

Very small samplers were often exchanged as gifts in the 18th and 19th centuries, personalized with initials and dates, a tradition which is well worth continuing today.

Pincushions, letter-cases and needlebooks were popular items made for the sales of work or bazaars that were introduced in the 1830s, and children working in schools of industry produced examples of very fine embroidery, which were sold for a few pence as souvenirs to visitors to the school.

For those readers who would like to make a small item, using a limited amount of time, canvas and thread, I have devised a selection of 'tokens' using borders and motifs. The choice of colours is, of course, unlimited, and you can easily adapt the designs by creating your own combination of motifs and borders.

Making up the 'tokens'

Simple pincushions Trim the canvas to within five double threads of the embroidery. Cut a piece of felt or linen to the same size. Tack the two pieces together, right sides facing. Machine or hand sew round three sides, leaving the fourth side open for stuffing. Trim the corners, turn right side out. Stuff with kapok, turn in the raw edges on the fourth side, and slipstitch together firmly.

Deep pincushion Cut away the canvas at the corners to within three double threads of the embroidery. On the wrong side, stitch the corners together using strong thread and taking the stitches into the last row of holes used for the embroidery so that no spare canvas shows on the right side. Cut a piece of felt or linen for the backing fabric and finish in the same way as for the two-sided pincushion.

Spectacle cases N.B. The same design is inverted to form the reverse side, and both sides are cut and stitched as one.

Trim the canvas to within five double threads of the embroidery. Pad the canvas slightly with fabric or wadding and turn in the unstitched edges of the canvas. Line with a piece of felt cut to size and slipstitched to the canvas. Fold the case in half along the bottom edge, and slipstitch the sides to finish.

If you prefer, you can stiffen the case by inserting a piece of thin cardboard, cut to size, between the canvas and the felt lining on the back of the case.

Comb case The front and back are cut and stitched as one, as for the spectacle cases, but in this case are joined down one side. Make up in the same way as for the spectacle cases, but omit the padding between the canvas and lining.

Paper tissues case The front of the case only is embroidered. Trim the canvas to within five single threads of the embroidery. Pad slightly with fabric or wadding, turn in the unstitched edges of the canvas and line with a piece of felt cut to size and slip-stitched in position. Cut another piece of felt to the same size and slipstitch to the lined piece on three sides to form a pocket.

Cigarette lighter case Make up as for the tissue case, and fasten with a press stud just inside the top edge.

Child's purse Trim the canvas to within five single threads of the embroidery. Line the embroidery with a piece of felt or fabric cut to size. Cut a piece of felt to the same size for the backing. Attach a zip equal in length to the width of the embroidered area to the top edge of the purse and one long edge of the felt. Open the zip, then join the front of the purse to the back with right sides facing. Turn the purse through to the right side.

Potholder Trim the canvas to within five double threads of the embroidery. Cut a piece of linen to the same size for the backing. With right sides facing, join the front to the back on three sides. Turn through to the right side, pad with fabric or wadding, and slipstitch the fourth side to close. Insert a loop made from linen at one of the corners from which to hang the potholder.

Egg cosies Make up as for the tissue case, but pad the front of the egg cosy between the canvas and the lining.

Needle-book Trim the canvas to within eight single threads of the embroidery. Cut a piece of fabric or felt to the same size for the backing. With right sides facing, join the front to the backing on three sides. Turn

through to the right side. Cut a piece of thin cardboard to fit between the front and the backing to stiffen the needle-book. Score lightly across the centre of the card with the point of a pair of scissors so that the book can be folded in half. Insert the card, then slipstitch the fourth side to close. Sew small pieces of flannel inside the needle-book to hold the needles, and attach a pearl shank button to one short edge and a button loop to the other to fasten.

'Housewife' to hold sewing equipment The 'housewife' rolls up to a size of approximately 10 cm×8.5 cm (4 in×3 in). Line with a silky fabric as for the needle-book, then fold one end of the 'housewife' to the inside to form a pocket 7.5 cm (3 in) deep. Slipstitch the sides to hold. Roll up, and attach three press studs in the correct positions to close.

Jewellery case Line the canvas with felt as for the needle-book, attaching three felt pockets with flaps and button fastenings to the lining. Attach a strip of felt at each end to tie into a bow to fasten the case.

Small picture You can make a simple frame for a very small sampler by cutting strips of balsa wood and gluing them together. Attach the sampler to the back of the frame with double-sided sellotape.

Paperweight You can buy square, rectangular or circular glass paperweights from good embroidery shops. Trim the canvas to within five double threads of the embroidery. Fold these edges to the back of the work and stitch or glue firmly in place. Secure to the glass at the edges, using strong adhesive. Glue a piece of felt, cut to size, to the bottom of the canvas to finish.

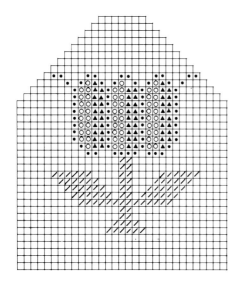

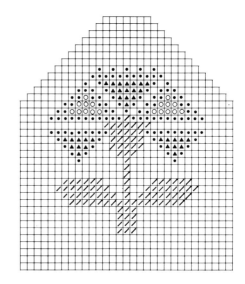

egg cosy

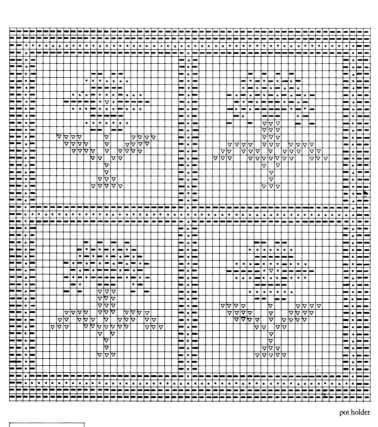

pot holder

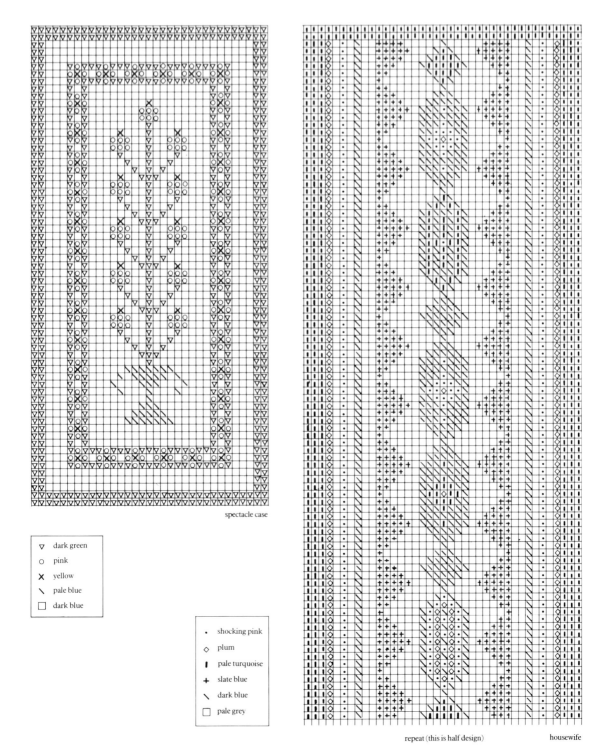

spectacle case

▽	dark green
○	pink
✗	yellow
╲	pale blue
☐	dark blue

•	shocking pink
◇	plum
❙	pale turquoise
✚	slate blue
╲	dark blue
☐	pale grey

repeat (this is half design)   housewife

71

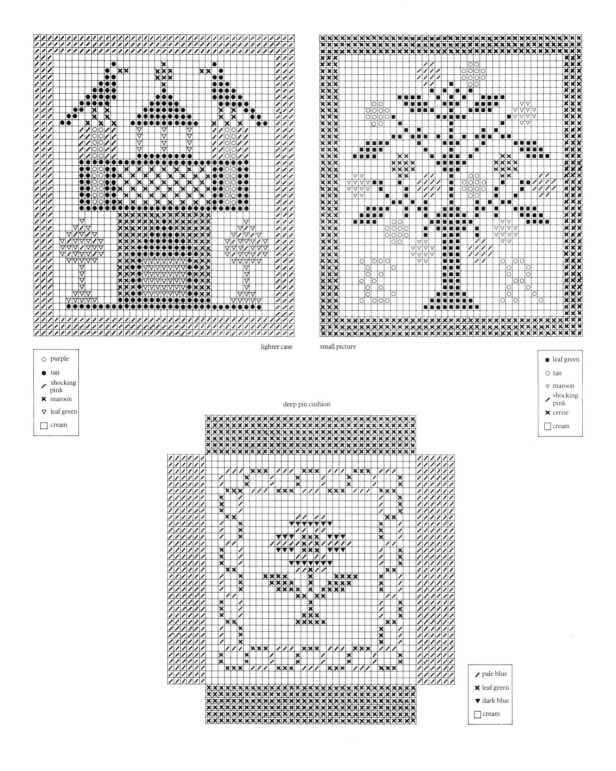

lighter case   small picture

deep pin cushion

lighter case / small picture legend

○ purple
● tan
╱ shocking pink
✕ maroon
▽ leaf green
☐ cream

small picture legend

■ leaf green
○ tan
▽ maroon
╱ shocking pink
✕ cerise
☐ cream

deep pin cushion legend

╱ pale blue
✕ leaf green
▼ dark blue
☐ cream

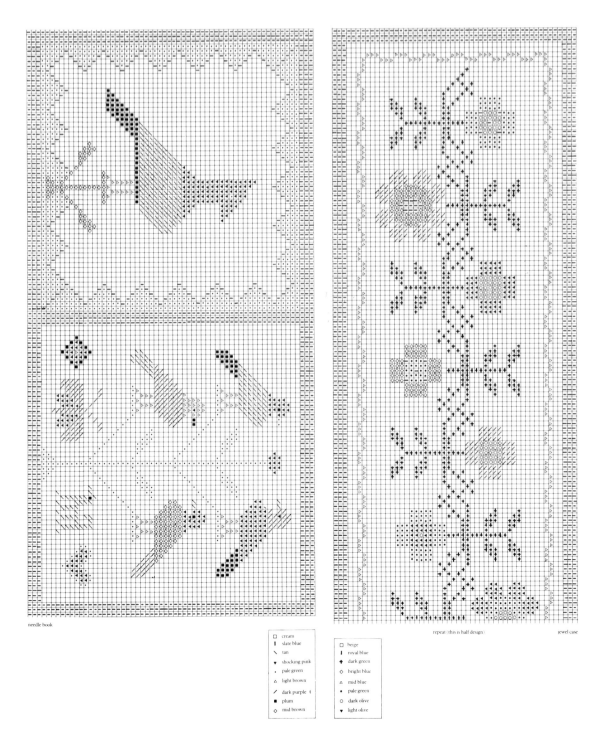

needle book

repeat (this is half design)   jewel case

	cream			beige
I	slate blue		I	royal blue
\	tan		♣	dark green
▼	shocking pink		◇	bright blue
·	pale green		▵	mid blue
▵	light brown		·	pale green
/	dark purple		○	dark olive
■	plum		▼	light olive
◇	mid brown			

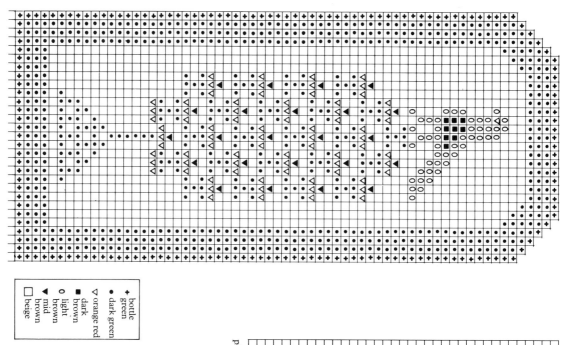

pin cushion

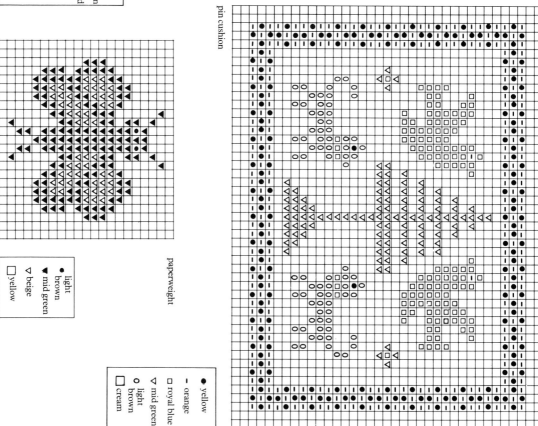

bottle
+ bottle green
• dark green
▽ orange red
■ dark brown
○ light brown
◀ mid brown
☐ beige

paperweight
• light brown
◀ mid green
▽ beige
☐ yellow

pin cushion
• yellow
− orange
☐ royal blue
▽ mid green
○ light brown
☐ cream

78

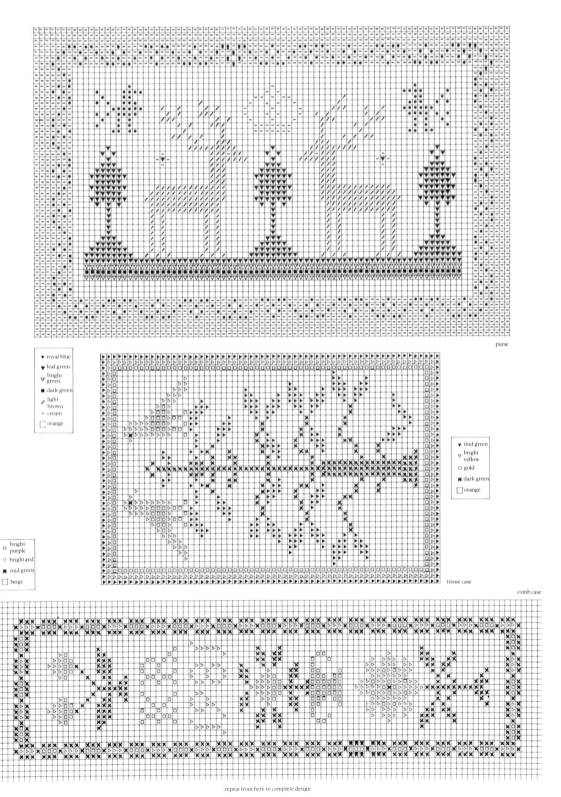

purse

- royal blue
- ▼ leaf green
- ▽ bright green
- ■ dark green
- ∕ light brown
- − cream
- ▢ orange

- ▼ mid green
- ∨ bright yellow
- ▢ gold
- ✹ dark green
- ▢ orange

tissue case

comb case

- ▢ bright purple
- ∨ bright red
- ✹ mid green
- ▢ beige

repeat from here to complete design

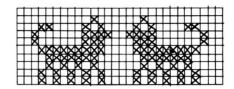

DESIGNING YOUR OWN SAMPLER

Having looked at the various photographs of historical samplers, you may want to create your own piece of work, perhaps to commemorate the date of a marriage with the names of the couple, the birth of a child or children, or just as a decorative piece of work.

Work the design out first on a piece of graph paper, before you begin to embroider. You can buy graph paper at most stationers, and 10 squares to 2.5 cm (1 in) is a good size to use.

The size of the sampler will obviously depend on how much you wish to include. If you are going to use lettering or numerals (see page 62), plan these first on the graph paper. You can then find out how much space they will occupy by counting the equivalent number of threads on your canvas. In the same way, you can calculate how much space you will need for motifs or a border, and how best to position them. You may find it necessary to shorten or extend the width and depth of your main design to make the border pattern dovetail at the corners.

The charted motifs on pages 83 to 95 have been drawn from notes made from samplers in museums, private collections and the homes of friends and relatives. Some samplers I have seen have been passed down through generations of families who proudly claim the name of the embroiderer to be that of a distant relative.

The motifs vary considerably in size and complexity. Use single motifs to fill space at the end of an alphabet, or between larger motifs.

Most of the animals, flowers and other motifs which appear on samplers have an historical or religious significance, and some of these are given on pages 27 to 28.

Verses, texts and inscriptions from 18th- and 19th-century samplers

The following examples convey sentiments on such diverse subjects as life, death, education, manners, religion, the duties of children to parents, the use of time and the worthy role of needlework. These verses and phrases have been collected from a wide range of samplers of different periods, and you can find other appropriate maxims in old-fashioned books on household lore, as well as texts from the Bible. If you are working a more modern sampler, you could equally well choose a modern text. Initials and date would be sufficient for a wedding sampler or a family tree.

For a longer inscription or verse, you will need to use a fine canvas – a four-line verse can take up a lot of space, even on a canvas with 12 single threads to 2.5 cm (1 in).

It is always a good idea to include a date on your sampler – it is surprising how quickly the skill and affection you have put into your piece of needlework can make it a treasured heirloom.

Make much of time.

Keep such company as you may improve or that may improve you.

Fear the Lord, Obey your Parents, Praise the Lord, Pray to God.

Always speak the truth.

That which will not make a pot may make a pot lid.

He who spends all he gets is on the high road to want.

A small hole will sink a great ship.

Show me the right way O Lord and guide me into it.

A diligent scholar is an ornament to a school.

Knowledge is a comfortable and necessary retreat and shelter for us in an advanced age, and if we do not plant it when young it will give us no shade when we grow old.

Trust ye in the Lord for ever, for in the Lord Jehovah is everlasting strength.

Compare the miseries on Earth with the Joys of Heaven and the length of one with the eternity of the other.

Never delay till tomorrow what reason and conscience tell you ought to be done today. Tomorrow is not yours and though you should live to enjoy it you must not overload it with a burden not its own. Sufficient for the day is the Business thereof.

If thou hast gathered nothing in thy youth How canst thou find anything in thine age?

She who is truly polite knows how to contradict with respect and please without adulation, is equally remote from insipid complaisance and low familiarity.

*Many daughters
have done virtuously,
but thou excellest
them all.*

*Give first to God the flower of thy youth.
Take for thy guide the blessed word of truth.*

*Scorn the deluding arts that most bewitches
And place thy hopes in everlasting riches.*

Glory to God
*To God the Father, God the Son
And God the Spirit Three in One,
Be Honour Praise and Glory given
By all on earth and all in Heaven.*

*'Tis religion that can give
Sweeetest pleasure while we live.
'Tis religion must supply
Solid comfort when we die.
After death its joy will be
Lasting as eternity.
Be the living God my friend
Then my bliss shall never end.*

*How blest are they who in their Prime
The paths of truth have early trod,
Who yield the first fruits of their time
And consecrate their youth to God.*

*Fear the Lord and He will be
A tender father unto thee.*

*When I can read my title clear
To mansions in the skies,
I'll bid farewell to every fear
And wipe my weeping eyes.*

*I sigh not for beauty nor languish for wealth
But grant me kind providence virtue and health
Then richer than kings and more happy than they
My days shall pass sweetly and swiftly away.*

A Friendly Wish
May heavenly Angels their soft wings display
And guide you safe through every dangerous
way,
In every place may you most happy be
And when you read my Wish pray think of
me.

The Lord my pasture shall prepare
And guard me with a shepherd's care,
His presence shall my wants supply
And guard me with a watchful eye.

Count that day lost, whose low descending sun
Views from thy hand no worthy action done.

See how the Lilies flourish white and fair
See how the ravens fed from Heaven are,
Then ne'er distrust the God for cloth and
Bread
Whilst lilies flourish and the Ravens fed.

The rising morning can't assure
That we shall end the day!
For death stands ready at the door
To take our lives away.

Not Land but Learning
Makes a Man complete
Not Birth but Breeding
Makes him truly Great
Not Wealth but Wisdom
Does adorn his State
Virtue not Honour
Makes him Fortunate.
Learning Breeding Wisdom
Get these three
Then Wealth and Honour
Will attend on thee.

O 'tis a folly and a crime
To put religion by
For now is the accepted time
Tomorrow we may die.

Save me lord from sin and fear
Bring thy great salvation near
Bring into my soul thy peace

Everlasting righteousness.

Best Use of Riches
When wealth to virtuous hands is giv'n
It blesses like the dews of heav'n
Like heav'n it hears the orphan's cries
And wipes the tears from widow's eyes.

Our life is never at a stand
'Tis like a fading flower
Death which is always near at hand
Comes nearer every hour.

Tell me ye knowing and discerning few
Where I may find a friend both firm and true
Who dares stand by me when in deep distress
And then his love and friendship most
express.

The Lord whose mercies never cease
Still crown our Families with peace
From Him the dear Connections rose
And all our Blessings He bestows.

Why those fears Behold this Jesus
Holds the helm, and guides the ship,
Spreads the sails to catch the breezes
Sent to waft us through the deep.
To the regions – to the regions
Where the mourners cease to weep.

Concerning Needlework
When this you see remember me
And keep it in your mind,
Let all the world say what they will
Speak of me as you find.

This have I done to let you see
What care my Parents took of me.

This work in hand my friends may have
When I am dead and laid in grave.

Of female arts in usefulness
The needle far exceeds the rest,
In ornament there's no device
Affords adorning half so nice.

82

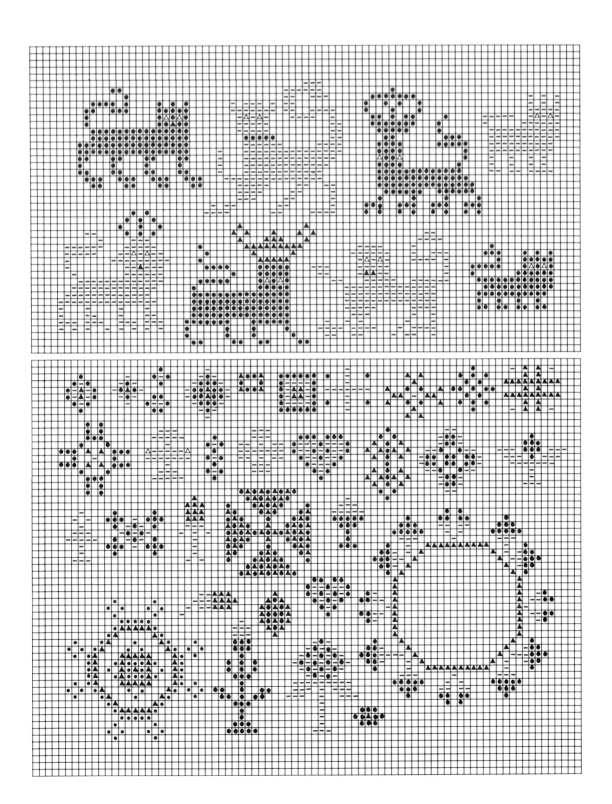

83

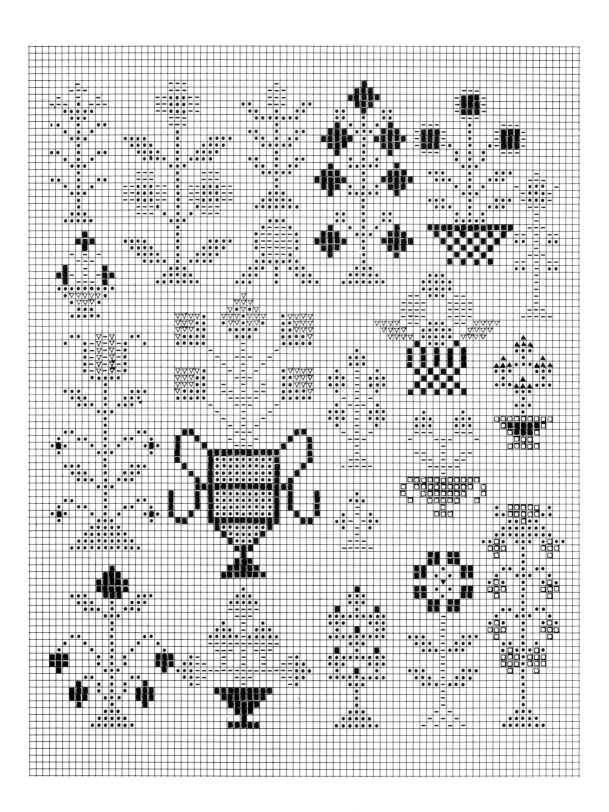

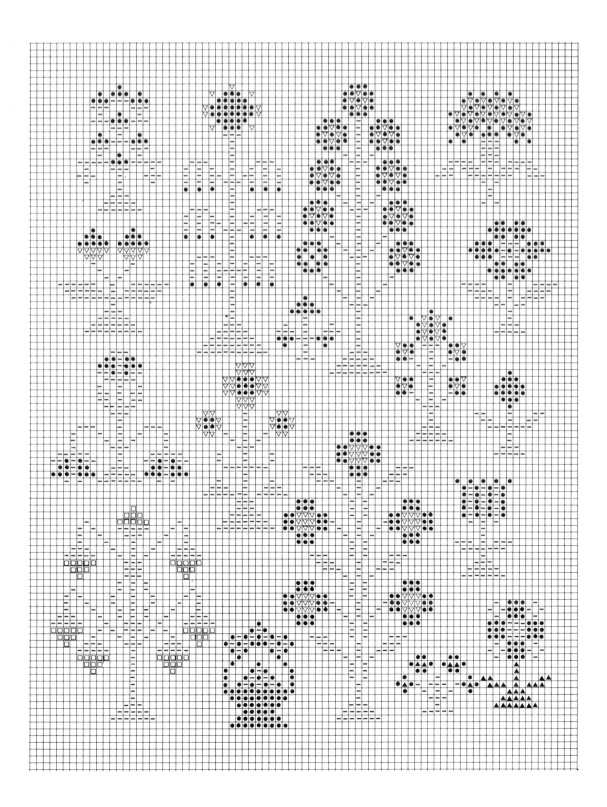

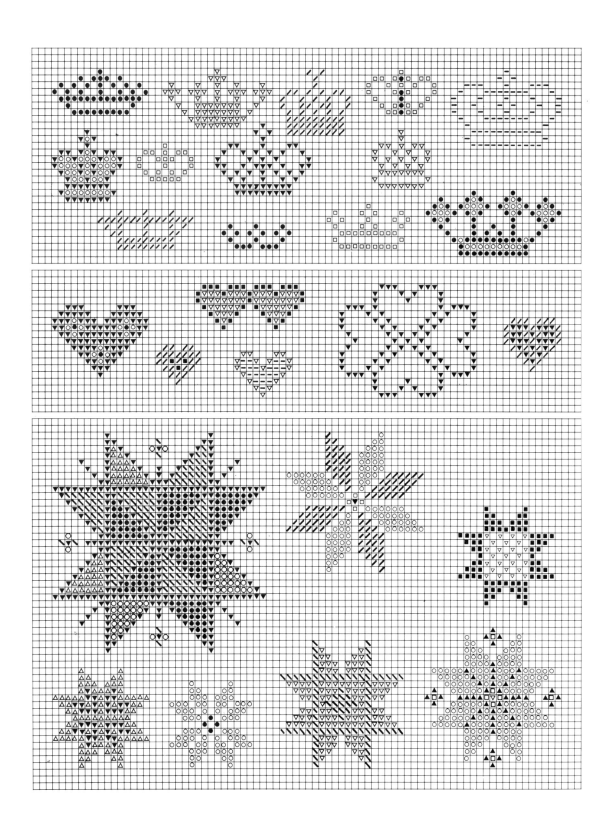

94

Where To See Samplers

Many museums have samplers in their collections but unfortunately, owing to lack of space, many samplers are stored out of sight of the general public. Most museum staff, however, given notice, are happy to show them to the interested visitor.

The following museums have collections which are well worth a visit if you are in the vicinity.

United Kingdom
Bristol City Museum, Bristol
Camphill Museum, Glasgow – *The Burrell Collection*; Castle Museum, Nottingham
Dorset County Museum, Dorchester
Fitzwilliam Museum, Cambridge
Gawthorpe Hall, Padiham, near Preston
Guildford Museum, Guildford
The Lady Lever Art Gallery, Port Sunlight, Merseyside
National Museum of Ireland, Dublin
National Museum of Wales (St Fagan's), Cardiff
Royal Scottish Museum, Edinburgh
Stranger's Hall Museum, Norwich
Ulster Folk Museum, Holywood, County Down
Victoria and Albert Museum, London
Wells Museum, Wells, Somerset

Denmark
Nationalmuseet, Copenhagen

Germany
Museum für Deutsche Volkskunde, West Berlin

Holland
Het Nederlands Openluchtmuseum, Arnhem

United States of America
Cooper-Hewitt Museum of Design (Smithsonian Institution), New York
Henry Francis du Pont Winterthur Museum, Winterthur, Delaware
Metropolitan Museum of Art, New York
Museum of American Folk Art, New York
National Museum of History & Technology (Smithsonian Institution), Washington D.C.
Philadelphia Museum of Art, Philadelphia. *The Whitman Sampler Collection*

List of Suppliers

When purchasing canvas, wool and embroidery frames, it is advisable to deal with a specialist shop. Most of these shops have a mail order service and supply a catalogue, and will usually give helpful advice to the beginner.

The Campden Needlecraft Centre, High Street, Chipping Campden, Gloucestershire

The Danish Embroidery Centre Ltd, The Old Rectory, Claydon, Ipswich, Suffolk IP6 0EQ

The Danish House, 16 Sloane Street, London SW1

de Denne Ltd, 159/161 Kenton Road, Kenton, Harrow, Middlesex

Ruth John Embroidery Materials, 39 The Square, Titchfield, Hampshire PO14 4AQ

The Ladies' Work Society, Delabere House, New Road, Moreton-in-Marsh, Gloucestershire

Mace & Nairn, 89 Crane Street, Salisbury, Wiltshire SP1 2PY

Ries Wools, 243 High Holborn, London WC1

Royal School of Needlework, 25 Princes Gate, London SW7 1QE

The Silver Thimble, 33 Gay Street, Bath, Avon BA1 2NT

Further Reading

Colby, Averil *Samplers* B. T. Batsford, London 1964
Green, Sylvia *Canvas Embroidery for Beginners* Studio Vista, London 1970
Horner, Marianna Merritt *The Story of Samplers* Philadelphia Museum of Art, Philadelphia 1963
Huish, Marcus *Samplers and Tapestry Embroideries* Longmans & Co. London 1900. Reprinted Dover Publications, New York 1963
Jones, Mary Eirwen *British Samplers* Pen-in-Hand, Oxford 1948
King, Donald *Samplers* Victoria and Albert Museum, London 1960
Krueger, Glee *A Gallery of American Samplers* E. P. Dutton in association with the Museum of American Folk Art, New York 1978
Meulenbelt-Nieuwburg, Albarta *Embroidery Motifs from Dutch Samplers* B. T. Batsford, London 1974
Proctor, Molly G. *Victorian Canvas Work: Berlin Wool Work* B. T. Batsford, London 1972
Sebba, Anne *Samplers, Five Centuries of a Gentle Craft* Weidenfeld & Nicolson, London 1979
Swan, Susan Burrows *Plain and Fancy: American Women and Their Needlework, 1700–1850* Holt, Rinehart & Winston, New York 1977